G000066152

THIS PLANNER BELONGS TO

_____

If found, please email

_____

PLANNER

CRYSTAL STINE

HARVEST HOUSE PUBLISHERS
EUGENE, OREGON

INTRODUCTION

Popular messages in faith-based circles tell us that we should slow down, rest, and care for our souls. On the other hand, the world is shouting at us to do more, be more, have more. As believers, how do we balance God's model for work and rest with the passions and talents He's given us?

In my book *Holy Hustle: Embracing a Work-Hard, Rest-Well Life*, I take readers on an encouraging journey to discover how the right mix of hard work and the right kind of rest add up to blessings that just might surprise and delight. Through personal stories, Scripture, and reader interaction, we learn that when we work hard on the things God is giving us to do for His glory and honor, our hustle enhances the kingdom.

From redeeming the word "hustle" to discovering our superpower of service, *Holy Hustle* is not just the story of how God has redefined success, failure, and rest in my life, but an exciting invitation for you to see the worth of your work through God's eyes as we examine the examples He has for us in Scripture.

But why *Holy Hustle*?

Hustle works 24/7, jogging along in high heels on busy city streets with a coffee in one hand and a phone in the other, ignoring everyone around her. She is ruthless about getting the job done and will do whatever it takes to make sure she shines brighter than the rest, even if it means pulling an all-nighter to finish another presentation or missing time with her family. Hustle believes she can do it on her own if she simply works harder, does more, and says yes to everything. She doesn't need anyone else to help her because she knows she has what it takes.

Holy takes long, quiet walks in prayer labyrinths and devours books on self-care, soul-care, and grace. She wakes up early to spend no less than 30 minutes in her quiet-time chair, stocking up on scented candles and buying Bibles with extra-wide margins for journaling. Holy doesn't understand why Hustle can't slow down and rest, and Hustle doesn't understand why Holy seems to be missing the opportunity to serve her family and community through work.

What if there was another way to live? A place where we can find ourselves embracing the work God has given us while honoring His command to rest?

The message of holy hustle isn't intended to pile on criticism, doubt, or anxiety. This message is meant to affirm, encourage, and challenge us—not to do more, but to live more.

The holy hustle we're talking about has nothing to do with striving, working 24/7, ignoring our families, or doubting the impact we'll have as we faithfully pursue our work. Holy hustle doesn't put pressure on us to perform; it invites us to a deeper relationship with the only One who can turn our small offerings into great gifts.

In the beginning, God worked for six days and called it good. He rested on day seven and called it holy. We are made for holy hustle.

Be who God created you to be, live it boldly.

My prayer is that readers of *Holy Hustle* will experience...

- renewed peace as they focus on serving, not striving
- reawakened potential as they ditch comparison and embrace community
- redefined purpose as they seek the roles God has for them

And as you use this planner, my prayer is that you will be encouraged by the Scripture you'll discover on these pages, that you'll be inspired as you set goals and participate in the activities, and that each month as you engage with the "heart check," you will find yourself growing closer to God and embrace the beautiful plan He has for your life.

This planner is designed to be used however you most need it. No one will be there to see how many activities you do or if you skip a month completely and pick it up when you find your planner in your closet under that pile you've been meaning to go through. Let this be a tool you can use as you connect with God, become more intentional about your work, make space for rest, and gather with your community.

You were created to work with enthusiasm for the right reasons—and you were also made with a need to rest. Discover the place where these two sides meet in holy hustle.

"Whatever you do, do it from the heart, as something done for the Lord and not for people."

Colossians 3:23

MEET CRYSTAL

Crystal Stine is a coffee-obsessed, word-loving, self-proclaimed "digital missionary" who is passionate about using the message of holy hustle to encourage, equip, and inspire women of all ages to embrace a work-hard, rest-well lifestyle that honors God. A writer for more than decade, Crystal is the author of three self-published books: a Bible study called *Work Hard, Rest Well; Holy Hustle;* and *Quieting the Shout of Should.* Whether she is drawing on her experiences in motherhood, years of corporate life, work in ministry, or a new stage God has her in, Crystal writes and speaks to let women know that they are exactly where God needs them, that their work matters, and that they are the best one for the job. Crystal is married to her high-school sweetheart, and they are raising their daughter in Pennsylvania.

You can connect with Crystal online at **crystalstine.me**, learn more about her book (and take a fun quiz) at **holyhustlebook.com**, join more than 100,000 people who have completed the free 10-day "Holy Hustle" devotional on YouVersion, or find her on Instagram **@crystalstine.**

MY DREAMS, PLANS, AND GOALS FOR THE YEAR

From Dreaming to Doing

Use these pages to record your dreams, goals, and plans for the coming year. Take some time to pray through the big things you would like to accomplish and record them under the "My Dreams" section. Then break them down into smaller baby steps in the "My 'Do' List" section. Each month you will have an opportunity to flip back to this page, track your progress, and set some new next steps.

MY DREAMS

MY "DO" LIST

My Prayer for the Year

Spend some time with God and write down your prayer for the year. Imagine placing this planner and your plans in His hands, seeking wisdom, courage, joy, boldness, peace, and contentment as you work and rest each day.

_____

_____

_____

_____

_____

_____

_____

_____

_____

_____

_____

_____

_____

_____

_____

_____

_____

_____

_____

_____

_____

_____

_____

_____

_____

_____

_____

_____

_____

_____

_____

_____

_____

_____

_____

_____

_____

_____

There is worth in our work when we do it for the honor and glory of God — and with a joyful heart.

Month:

SUNDAY	MONDAY	TUESDAY	WEDNESDAY
———	———	———	———
———	———	———	———
———	———	———	———
———	———	———	———
———	———	———	———

LAZY   WORKING HARD / RESTING WELL   STRIVING

Mark a spot on this scale to indicate how you're feeling at the beginning of this month. Ask God to encourage, equip, or inspire you to find your way to the place where you can work hard and rest well.

Heart Check

THURSDAY	FRIDAY	SATURDAY	MY FOCUS FOR THE MONTH
___	___	___	
___	___	___	
___	___	___	
___	___	___	
___	___	___	

Month:

SUNDAY	MONDAY	TUESDAY	WEDNESDAY
_____	_____	_____	_____
_____	_____	_____	_____
_____	_____	_____	_____
_____	_____	_____	_____
_____	_____	_____	_____

LAZY　　　WORKING HARD / RESTING WELL　　　STRIVING

Mark a spot on this scale to indicate how you're feeling at the beginning of this month. Ask God to encourage, equip, or inspire you to find your way to the place where you can work hard and rest well.

THURSDAY	FRIDAY	SATURDAY	MY FOCUS FOR THE MONTH
——	——	——	
——	——	——	
——	——	——	
——	——	——	
——	——	——	

Month:

SUNDAY	MONDAY	TUESDAY	WEDNESDAY
____	____	____	____
____	____	____	____
____	____	____	____
____	____	____	____
____	____	____	____

Heart Check

Mark a spot on this scale to indicate how you're feeling at the beginning of this month. Ask God to encourage, equip, or inspire you to find your way to the place where you can work hard and rest well.

THURSDAY	FRIDAY	SATURDAY	MY FOCUS FOR THE MONTH
____	____	____	
____	____	____	
____	____	____	
____	____	____	
____	____	____	

Month:

SUNDAY	MONDAY	TUESDAY	WEDNESDAY
___	___	___	___
___	___	___	___
___	___	___	___
___	___	___	___
___	___	___	___

Heart Check

Mark a spot on this scale to indicate how you're feeling at the beginning of this month. Ask God to encourage, equip, or inspire you to find your way to the place where you can work hard and rest well.

THURSDAY	FRIDAY	SATURDAY	
——	——	——	**MY FOCUS FOR THE MONTH**
——	——	——	
——	——	——	
——	——	——	
——	——	——	

Month:

SUNDAY	MONDAY	TUESDAY	WEDNESDAY
_____	_____	_____	_____
_____	_____	_____	_____
_____	_____	_____	_____
_____	_____	_____	_____
_____	_____	_____	_____

LAZY   WORKING HARD / RESTING WELL   STRIVING

Heart Check

Mark a spot on this scale to indicate how you're feeling at the beginning of this month. Ask God to encourage, equip, or inspire you to find your way to the place where you can work hard and rest well.

THURSDAY	FRIDAY	SATURDAY	MY FOCUS FOR THE MONTH
___	___	___	
___	___	___	
___	___	___	
___	___	___	
___	___	___	

Month:

SUNDAY	MONDAY	TUESDAY	WEDNESDAY
____	____	____	____
____	____	____	____
____	____	____	____
____	____	____	____
____	____	____	____

LAZY   WORKING HARD / RESTING WELL   STRIVING

Heart Check

Mark a spot on this scale to indicate how you're feeling at the beginning of this month. Ask God to encourage, equip, or inspire you to find your way to the place where you can work hard and rest well.

THURSDAY	FRIDAY	SATURDAY	
_____	_____	_____	**MY FOCUS FOR THE MONTH**
_____	_____	_____	
_____	_____	_____	
_____	_____	_____	
_____	_____	_____	

Month:

SUNDAY	MONDAY	TUESDAY	WEDNESDAY
____	____	____	____
____	____	____	____
____	____	____	____
____	____	____	____
____	____	____	____

LAZY   WORKING HARD / RESTING WELL   STRIVING

Heart Check

Mark a spot on this scale to indicate how you're feeling at the beginning of this month. Ask God to encourage, equip, or inspire you to find your way to the place where you can work hard and rest well.

THURSDAY	FRIDAY	SATURDAY	MY FOCUS FOR THE MONTH
———	———	———	
———	———	———	
———	———	———	
———	———	———	
———	———	———	

Month:

SUNDAY	MONDAY	TUESDAY	WEDNESDAY
____	____	____	____
____	____	____	____
____	____	____	____
____	____	____	____
____	____	____	____

LAZY   WORKING HARD / RESTING WELL   STRIVING

Mark a spot on this scale to indicate how you're feeling at the beginning of this month. Ask God to encourage, equip, or inspire you to find your way to the place where you can work hard and rest well.

Heart Check

THURSDAY	FRIDAY	SATURDAY	MY FOCUS FOR THE MONTH
___	___	___	
___	___	___	
___	___	___	
___	___	___	
___	___	___	

Month:

SUNDAY	MONDAY	TUESDAY	WEDNESDAY
———	———	———	———
———	———	———	———
———	———	———	———
———	———	———	———
———	———	———	———

Mark a spot on this scale to indicate how you're feeling at the beginning of this month. Ask God to encourage, equip, or inspire you to find your way to the place where you can work hard and rest well.

THURSDAY	FRIDAY	SATURDAY	MY FOCUS FOR THE MONTH
___	___	___	
___	___	___	
___	___	___	
___	___	___	
___	___	___	

Month:

SUNDAY	MONDAY	TUESDAY	WEDNESDAY
____	____	____	____
____	____	____	____
____	____	____	____
____	____	____	____
____	____	____	____

LAZY   WORKING HARD / RESTING WELL   STRIVING

Mark a spot on this scale to indicate how you're feeling at the beginning of this month. Ask God to encourage, equip, or inspire you to find your way to the place where you can work hard and rest well.

THURSDAY	FRIDAY	SATURDAY	MY FOCUS FOR THE MONTH
___	___	___	
___	___	___	
___	___	___	
___	___	___	
___	___	___	

Month:

SUNDAY	MONDAY	TUESDAY	WEDNESDAY
_____	_____	_____	_____
_____	_____	_____	_____
_____	_____	_____	_____
_____	_____	_____	_____
_____	_____	_____	_____

Heart Check

Mark a spot on this scale to indicate how you're feeling at the beginning of this month. Ask God to encourage, equip, or inspire you to find your way to the place where you can work hard and rest well.

THURSDAY	FRIDAY	SATURDAY	MY FOCUS FOR THE MONTH
___	___	___	
___	___	___	
___	___	___	
___	___	___	
___	___	___	

Month:

SUNDAY	MONDAY	TUESDAY	WEDNESDAY
_____	_____	_____	_____
_____	_____	_____	_____
_____	_____	_____	_____
_____	_____	_____	_____
_____	_____	_____	_____

LAZY   WORKING HARD / RESTING WELL   STRIVING

Mark a spot on this scale to indicate how you're feeling at the beginning of this month. Ask God to encourage, equip, or inspire you to find your way to the place where you can work hard and rest well.

Heart Check

THURSDAY	FRIDAY	SATURDAY	MY FOCUS FOR THE MONTH
____	____	____	
____	____	____	
____	____	____	
____	____	____	
____	____	____	

TO DO

- ○
- ○
- ○
- ○
- ○
- ○
- ○
- ○
- ○
- ○
- ○
- ○
- ○

"Therefore, my dear brothers and sisters, *be steadfast, immovable,* always excelling in the *Lord's work,* because you know that your labor in the Lord is not in vain."

1 Corinthians 15:58

CHALLENGE:

Visit **holyhustlebook.com** and take the quiz to see where you fall on the holy hustle scale.

NOTES

Month:

MONDAY ____

TUESDAY ____

WEDNESDAY ____

THURSDAY ____

FRIDAY ____

SATURDAY ____

SUNDAY ____

TO DO

○
○
○
○
○
○
○
○
○
○
○
○

Putting others first isn't a problem - it's the whole point.

NOTES

PEOPLE TO ENCOURAGE

Month:

MONDAY _____

TUESDAY _____

WEDNESDAY _____

THURSDAY _____

FRIDAY _____

SATURDAY _____

SUNDAY _____

TO DO

- ○
- ○
- ○
- ○
- ○
- ○
- ○
- ○
- ○
- ○
- ○
- ○

"My salvation and glory depend on God, my strong rock. My refuge is in God."

Psalm 62:7

REFLECTION QUESTION:

How does your current state of busyness contribute to the work God has given you to do?

NOTES

Month:

MONDAY _____

TUESDAY _____

WEDNESDAY _____

THURSDAY _____

FRIDAY _____

SATURDAY _____

SUNDAY _____

TO DO

- ○
- ○
- ○
- ○
- ○
- ○
- ○
- ○
- ○
- ○
- ○
- ○

Plant seeds in faith and trust God in the harvest.

NOTES

PEOPLE TO PRAY FOR

Month:

MONDAY ____

TUESDAY ____

WEDNESDAY ____

THURSDAY ____

FRIDAY ____

SATURDAY ____

SUNDAY ____

TO DO

○
○
○
○
○
○
○
○
○
○
○
○

"Do not despise these small beginnings, for the LORD rejoices to see the work begin."

Zechariah 4:10 NLT

CHALLENGE:

Consider starting a book club with your friends.
Flip to the back of this planner and find out
how to start with *Holy Hustle*!

NOTES

Month:

MONDAY _____

TUESDAY _____

WEDNESDAY _____

THURSDAY _____

FRIDAY _____

SATURDAY _____

SUNDAY _____

TO DO

○
○
○
○
○
○
○
○
○
○
○
○

When we use our gifts to serve instead of strive, we find peace in the role God has given us.

NOTES

PEOPLE TO ENCOURAGE

Month:

MONDAY ____

TUESDAY ____

WEDNESDAY ____

THURSDAY ____

FRIDAY ____

SATURDAY ____

SUNDAY ____

TO DO

○
○
○
○
○
○
○
○
○
○
○
○

"I love you, LORD, my strength."

Psalm 18:1

REFLECTION QUESTION:

In what areas of your life has striving caused brokenness?

NOTES

Month: _____

MONDAY _____

TUESDAY _____

WEDNESDAY _____

THURSDAY _____

FRIDAY _____

SATURDAY _____ | **SUNDAY** _____

TO DO

○
○
○
○
○
○
○
○
○
○
○
○

We are symbols of hope, safe places to land on hard days, and friends who love deeply.

NOTES

PEOPLE TO PRAY FOR

Month:

MONDAY ____

TUESDAY ____

WEDNESDAY ____

THURSDAY ____

FRIDAY ____

SATURDAY ____

SUNDAY ____

TO DO

- ○
- ○
- ○
- ○
- ○
- ○
- ○
- ○
- ○
- ○
- ○
- ○

"Whatever your hands find to do, do with all your strength."

Ecclesiastes 9:10

CHALLENGE:

Use one of the gifts God has given you to volunteer in your church or community.

NOTES

Month:

MONDAY ____

TUESDAY ____

WEDNESDAY ____

THURSDAY ____

FRIDAY ____

SATURDAY ____

SUNDAY ____

TO DO

○
○
○
○
○
○
○
○
○
○
○
○
○

People over programs. Faith over fame. God's glory over success.

NOTES

PEOPLE TO ENCOURAGE

Month:

MONDAY _____

TUESDAY _____

WEDNESDAY _____

THURSDAY _____

FRIDAY _____

SATURDAY _____

SUNDAY _____

TO DO

○

○

○

○

○

○

○

○

○

○

○

○

"The LORD is my
strength and my song;
he has become my salvation.
This is my God, and
I will *praise* him,
my father's God, and
I will *exalt* him."

Exodus 15:2

REFLECTION QUESTION:

How has God blessed your
work in the past? How does
this encourage you to keep
moving forward today?

NOTES

Month:

MONDAY _____

TUESDAY _____

WEDNESDAY _____

THURSDAY _____

FRIDAY _____

SATURDAY _____

SUNDAY _____

TO DO

○
○
○
○
○
○
○
○
○
○
○
○

God will use every piece of our story to illuminate His glory.

NOTES

PEOPLE TO PRAY FOR

Month:

MONDAY _____

TUESDAY _____

WEDNESDAY _____

THURSDAY _____

FRIDAY _____

SATURDAY _____

SUNDAY _____

TO DO

○
○
○
○
○
○
○
○
○
○
○
○
○

"*Love one another deeply as brothers and sisters. Outdo one another in showing honor.*"

Romans 12:10

CHALLENGE:

Share your testimony with someone who needs
to know about the hope you have in Jesus.

NOTES

Month:

MONDAY ____

TUESDAY ____

WEDNESDAY ____

THURSDAY ____

FRIDAY ____

SATURDAY ____

SUNDAY ____

TO DO

○
○
○
○
○
○
○
○
○
○
○
○

Everyone has work to do that honors God.

NOTES

PEOPLE TO ENCOURAGE

Month:

MONDAY ____

TUESDAY ____

WEDNESDAY ____

THURSDAY ____

FRIDAY ____

SATURDAY ____ | **SUNDAY** ____

TO DO

- ○
- ○
- ○
- ○
- ○
- ○
- ○
- ○
- ○
- ○
- ○
- ○
- ○

"You are saved by
grace through faith, and
this is not from yourselves;
it is God's gift—not from works,
so that no one can boast.
For we are his workmanship,
created in Christ Jesus for
good works, which God
prepared ahead of time
for us to do."

Ephesians 2:8-10

REFLECTION QUESTION:

Have you ever doubted your
calling, significance, or purpose?
How does knowing you're not
enough—but God is—help you
embrace holy hustle?

NOTES

Month:

MONDAY _____

TUESDAY _____

WEDNESDAY _____

THURSDAY _____

FRIDAY _____

SATURDAY _____

SUNDAY _____

TO DO

○

○

○

○

○

○

○

○

○

○

○

○

Trust God to do a new thing.

NOTES

PEOPLE TO PRAY FOR

Month:

MONDAY _____

TUESDAY _____

WEDNESDAY _____

THURSDAY _____

FRIDAY _____

SATURDAY _____ | **SUNDAY** _____

TO DO

○
○
○
○
○
○
○
○
○
○
○
○
○

"The LORD is my
shepherd;
I have what I need.

He lets me lie down in
green pastures;
he leads me beside
quiet waters.
He renews my life;

he leads me along the
right paths
for his name's sake."

Psalm 23:1-3

CHALLENGE:

Feeling stretched too thin or need some creative inspiration?
Go for a walk or work in a new place. Sometimes a change
of scenery can kick-start new ideas!

NOTES

Month:

MONDAY _____

TUESDAY _____

WEDNESDAY _____

THURSDAY _____

FRIDAY _____

SATURDAY _____

SUNDAY _____

TO DO

○
○
○
○
○
○
○
○
○
○
○
○

God called His work "good," and He called rest "holy."

NOTES

PEOPLE TO ENCOURAGE

Month:

MONDAY ____

TUESDAY ____

WEDNESDAY ____

THURSDAY ____

FRIDAY ____

SATURDAY ____

SUNDAY ____

TO DO

○
○
○
○
○
○
○
○
○
○
○
○

"Do not be
conformed to this age,
but be *transformed* by
the renewing of your mind,
so that you may discern
what is the good, pleasing,
and *perfect* will
of God."

Romans 12:2

REFLECTION QUESTION:

If tomorrow was your only day
to use the talents God gave
you, what would you do?

NOTES

Month: ____

MONDAY ____

TUESDAY ____

WEDNESDAY ____

THURSDAY ____

FRIDAY ____

SATURDAY ____

SUNDAY ____

TO DO

○
○
○
○
○
○
○
○
○
○
○
○

Work hard,
rest well.

NOTES

PEOPLE TO PRAY FOR

Month:

MONDAY _____

TUESDAY _____

WEDNESDAY _____

THURSDAY _____

FRIDAY _____

SATURDAY _____

SUNDAY _____

TO DO

○
○
○
○
○
○
○
○
○
○
○
○

"*Friends*, don't get me wrong:
By no means do I count myself
an expert in all of this, but
I've got my *eye on the goal*,
where God is beckoning us
onward—to Jesus.
I'm off and running,
and I'm not turning back."

Philippians 3:13-14
(MSG)

CHALLENGE:

Take a step back from your work and ask God to
renew and transform your mind.

NOTES

Month:

MONDAY ____

TUESDAY ____

WEDNESDAY ____

THURSDAY ____

FRIDAY ____

SATURDAY ____ | **SUNDAY** ____

TO DO

- ○
- ○
- ○
- ○
- ○
- ○
- ○
- ○
- ○
- ○
- ○
- ○

When we show up to work, God will work out His plan for our lives.

NOTES

PEOPLE TO ENCOURAGE

Month:

MONDAY _____

TUESDAY _____

WEDNESDAY _____

THURSDAY _____

FRIDAY _____

SATURDAY _____

SUNDAY _____

TO DO

○
○
○
○
○
○
○
○
○
○
○
○

"Watch closely: I am preparing something *new*; it's happening now, *even as I speak,* and you're about to see it. I am preparing *a way through the desert*; waters will flow where there had been none."

Isaiah 43:19
(VOICE)

REFLECTION QUESTION:

What space have you been avoiding because you don't feel good enough?

NOTES

Month:

MONDAY _____

TUESDAY _____

WEDNESDAY _____

THURSDAY _____

FRIDAY _____

SATURDAY _____

SUNDAY _____

TO DO

○
○
○
○
○
○
○
○
○
○
○
○

Holy hustle means making God's name great, not our own.

NOTES

PEOPLE TO PRAY FOR

Month:

MONDAY ____

TUESDAY ____

WEDNESDAY ____

THURSDAY ____

FRIDAY ____

SATURDAY ____

SUNDAY ____

TO DO

○
○
○
○
○
○
○
○
○
○
○
○

"There has never been
the slightest doubt in my
mind that the God who
started this *great work*
in you would keep at it and
bring it to a flourishing
finish on the very day
Christ Jesus appears."

Philippians 1:6
(MSG)

CHALLENGE:

Use your superpower of service to invest in your family,
community, neighbors, workplace, or church.

NOTES

Month:

MONDAY ____

TUESDAY ____

WEDNESDAY ____

THURSDAY ____

FRIDAY ____

SATURDAY ____

SUNDAY ____

TO DO

○
○
○
○
○
○
○
○
○
○
○
○

Holy hustle is only and always about shining the spotlight on God.

NOTES

PEOPLE TO ENCOURAGE

Month:

MONDAY _____

TUESDAY _____

WEDNESDAY _____

THURSDAY _____

FRIDAY _____

SATURDAY _____

SUNDAY _____

TO DO

○
○
○
○
○
○
○
○
○
○
○
○

"Her shining light will not be extinguished, no matter how dark the night."

Proverbs 31:18 TPT

REFLECTION QUESTION:

How has God been nudging your heart, affirming your gifts, encouraging your dreams, and using you in small, ordinary, faith-filled, and fame-free moments?

NOTES

Month:

MONDAY ____

TUESDAY ____

WEDNESDAY ____

THURSDAY ____

FRIDAY ____

SATURDAY ____

SUNDAY ____

TO DO

○
○
○
○
○
○
○
○
○
○
○
○

What you begin in faith, God will finish with a flourish.

NOTES

PEOPLE TO PRAY FOR

Month:

MONDAY _____

TUESDAY _____

WEDNESDAY _____

THURSDAY _____

FRIDAY _____

SATURDAY _____

SUNDAY _____

TO DO

○
○
○
○
○
○
○
○
○
○
○
○

"You are a chosen race,
a royal priesthood,
a holy nation, a people
for his possession, so that you
may *proclaim* the praises of
the one who called you
out of darkness into his
marvelous light."

1 Peter 2:9

CHALLENGE:

Outdo someone in showing honor—
even if it means putting them first.

NOTES

Month:

MONDAY _____

TUESDAY _____

WEDNESDAY _____

THURSDAY _____

FRIDAY _____

SATURDAY _____

SUNDAY _____

TO DO

○
○
○
○
○
○
○
○
○
○
○
○

Invest in learning, not assuming, so you can be encouraging, not envious.

NOTES

PEOPLE TO ENCOURAGE

Month:

MONDAY _____

TUESDAY _____

WEDNESDAY _____

THURSDAY _____

FRIDAY _____

SATURDAY _____

SUNDAY _____

TO DO

○

○

○

○

○

○

○

○

○

○

○

○

"Look, I have inscribed you on the palms of my hands; your walls are continually before me."

Isaiah 49:16

REFLECTION QUESTION:

What parts of your plan are you holding on to instead of handing them over to God?

NOTES

Month:

MONDAY _____

TUESDAY _____

WEDNESDAY _____

THURSDAY _____

FRIDAY _____

SATURDAY _____

SUNDAY _____

TO DO

○

○

○

○

○

○

○

○

○

○

○

○

God has a plan for you, right where you are.

NOTES

PEOPLE TO PRAY FOR

Month:

MONDAY ____

TUESDAY ____

WEDNESDAY ____

THURSDAY ____

FRIDAY ____

SATURDAY ____

SUNDAY ____

TO DO

○
○
○
○
○
○
○
○
○
○
○
○

*"Be still,
and know
that I am
God"*

Psalm 46:10 NIV

CHALLENGE:

Spend time in prayer, asking God to show you where
you've been competing instead of collaborating.

NOTES

Month:

MONDAY _____

TUESDAY _____

WEDNESDAY _____

THURSDAY _____

FRIDAY _____

SATURDAY _____

SUNDAY _____

TO DO

○
○
○
○
○
○
○
○
○
○
○
○

We're not meant to be famous—We're meant to make God famous.

NOTES

PEOPLE TO ENCOURAGE

Month:

MONDAY _____

TUESDAY _____

WEDNESDAY _____

THURSDAY _____

FRIDAY _____

SATURDAY _____

SUNDAY _____

TO DO

○
○
○
○
○
○
○
○
○
○
○
○

*"She came and
has been on her feet
since early morning,
except that she
rested a little in
the shelter."*

Ruth 2:7

REFLECTION QUESTION:

What is it that truly
brings you rest?

NOTES

Month:

MONDAY _____

TUESDAY _____

WEDNESDAY _____

THURSDAY _____

FRIDAY _____

SATURDAY _____

SUNDAY _____

TO DO

○

○

○

○

○

○

○

○

○

○

○

○

Our small act of obedience can make a significant impact in God's kingdom.

NOTES

PEOPLE TO PRAY FOR

Month:

MONDAY _____

TUESDAY _____

WEDNESDAY _____

THURSDAY _____

FRIDAY _____

SATURDAY _____ | **SUNDAY** _____

TO DO

○
○
○
○
○
○
○
○
○
○
○
○

"LORD, you light my lamp; my God illuminates my darkness."

Psalm 18:28

CHALLENGE:

Find a way to let your light shine in a new place—
your light isn't meant to be hidden.

NOTES

Month:

MONDAY _____

TUESDAY _____

WEDNESDAY _____

THURSDAY _____

FRIDAY _____

SATURDAY _____

SUNDAY _____

TO DO

○
○
○
○
○
○
○
○
○
○
○
○

Wait expectantly.

NOTES

PEOPLE TO ENCOURAGE

Month:

MONDAY ____

TUESDAY ____

WEDNESDAY ____

THURSDAY ____

FRIDAY ____

SATURDAY ____ | **SUNDAY** ____

TO DO

○
○
○
○
○
○
○
○
○
○
○
○

"I, the prisoner in the Lord, urge you to live *worthy* of the calling you have received, with all *humility* and gentleness, with patience, bearing with one another in *love*, making every effort to keep the unity of the Spirit through the *bond of peace*."

Ephesians 4:1-3

REFLECTION QUESTION:

What are your motivations behind your work and the goals you've set?

NOTES

Month:

MONDAY ____

TUESDAY ____

WEDNESDAY ____

THURSDAY ____

FRIDAY ____

SATURDAY ____

SUNDAY ____

TO DO

○

○

○

○

○

○

○

○

○

○

○

○

*Not every door
is meant for us.
Not every door
leads us home.*

NOTES

PEOPLE TO PRAY FOR

Month:

MONDAY _____

TUESDAY _____

WEDNESDAY _____

THURSDAY _____

FRIDAY _____

SATURDAY _____

SUNDAY _____

TO DO

○
○
○
○
○
○
○
○
○
○
○
○
○

"The LORD is my *strength* and my *shield*; my heart trusts in him, and I am helped. Therefore my heart celebrates, and I *give thanks* to him with my song."

Psalm 28:7

CHALLENGE:

Make a list of things that bring your heart joy or rest and incorporate one thing into your schedule.

NOTES

Month:

MONDAY _____

TUESDAY _____

WEDNESDAY _____

THURSDAY _____

FRIDAY _____

SATURDAY _____

SUNDAY _____

TO DO

- ○
- ○
- ○
- ○
- ○
- ○
- ○
- ○
- ○
- ○
- ○
- ○
- ○

We are not called to the easy life, but to a holy life.

NOTES

PEOPLE TO ENCOURAGE

Month:

MONDAY _____

TUESDAY _____

WEDNESDAY _____

THURSDAY _____

FRIDAY _____

SATURDAY _____

SUNDAY _____

TO DO

○
○
○
○
○
○
○
○
○
○
○
○

"Your word is a
lamp for my feet
and a light on
my path."

Psalm 119:105

REFLECTION QUESTION:

If rest is hard for you,
what are you afraid will
happen if you step away
from the work?

NOTES

Month:

MONDAY _____

TUESDAY _____

WEDNESDAY _____

THURSDAY _____

FRIDAY _____

SATURDAY _____

SUNDAY _____

TO DO

○

○

○

○

○

○

○

○

○

○

○

○

○

What God has spoken to you in the light should not be doubted in the dark.

NOTES

PEOPLE TO PRAY FOR

Month:

MONDAY ____

TUESDAY ____

WEDNESDAY ____

THURSDAY ____

FRIDAY ____

SATURDAY ____

SUNDAY ____

TO DO

○

○

○

○

○

○

○

○

○

○

○

○

"We plan the way we want to live, but only GOD makes us able to live it."

Proverbs 16:9 MSG

CHALLENGE:

Practice saying no to things that
aren't meant for you.

NOTES

Month:

MONDAY _____

TUESDAY _____

WEDNESDAY _____

THURSDAY _____

FRIDAY _____

SATURDAY _____

SUNDAY _____

TO DO

○
○
○
○
○
○
○
○
○
○
○
○

The work God has called us to do is worth the cost.

NOTES

PEOPLE TO ENCOURAGE

Month:

MONDAY ____

TUESDAY ____

WEDNESDAY ____

THURSDAY ____

FRIDAY ____

SATURDAY ____

SUNDAY ____

TO DO

- ◯
- ◯
- ◯
- ◯
- ◯
- ◯
- ◯
- ◯
- ◯
- ◯
- ◯
- ◯
- ◯

"Even the hairs of your head have all been counted."

Matthew 10:30

REFLECTION QUESTION:

What is one thing you can do this week to center yourself into that sweet spot of holy hustle?

NOTES

Month:

MONDAY ____

TUESDAY ____

WEDNESDAY ____

THURSDAY ____

FRIDAY ____

SATURDAY ____

SUNDAY ____

TO DO

- ◯
- ◯
- ◯
- ◯
- ◯
- ◯
- ◯
- ◯
- ◯
- ◯
- ◯
- ◯

Choose a life of faith even if it never brings fame.

NOTES

PEOPLE TO PRAY FOR

Month:

MONDAY _____

TUESDAY _____

WEDNESDAY _____

THURSDAY _____

FRIDAY _____

SATURDAY _____

SUNDAY _____

TO DO

○
○
○
○
○
○
○
○
○
○
○
○

"What an honor for me in GOD'S eyes! That God should be my strength!"

Isaiah 49:5 MSG

CHALLENGE:

Write down the ways God has answered your prayers or encouraged you this year so that later, when you need a reminder, you can look back and praise Him for His faithfulness.

NOTES

Month:

MONDAY _____

TUESDAY _____

WEDNESDAY _____

THURSDAY _____

FRIDAY _____

SATURDAY _____

SUNDAY _____

TO DO

○
○
○
○
○
○
○
○
○
○
○
○

You are irreplaceable, perfectly equipped, and incredibly necessary for the work God has planned for you.

NOTES

PEOPLE TO ENCOURAGE

Month:

MONDAY ____

TUESDAY ____

WEDNESDAY ____

THURSDAY ____

FRIDAY ____

SATURDAY ____

SUNDAY ____

TO DO

○
○
○
○
○
○
○
○
○
○
○
○

"So then, just as
you have received
Christ Jesus as Lord,
continue to walk in him,
being rooted and
built up in him and
established in the faith,
just as you were taught,
and overflowing
with *gratitude.*"

Colossians 2:6-7

REFLECTION QUESTION:

Where is God asking
you to trust Him and see
the work you've done as
good—even if it doesn't
feel finished?

NOTES

Month:

MONDAY _____

TUESDAY _____

WEDNESDAY _____

THURSDAY _____

FRIDAY _____

SATURDAY _____

SUNDAY _____

TO DO

○
○
○
○
○
○
○
○
○
○
○
○

*In Christ,
we can do more
than we could
ever imagine.*

NOTES

PEOPLE TO PRAY FOR

Month:

MONDAY _____

TUESDAY _____

WEDNESDAY _____

THURSDAY _____

FRIDAY _____

SATURDAY _____

SUNDAY _____

A *holy hustle* READING PLAN

When I wrote *Holy Hustle*, I had two important goals. I wanted the book to be full of Scripture so that your reading experience would become less about hearing my story and more about discovering the next steps God wants you to take in your own journey. It's why I also wrote *Work Hard, Rest Well*—an eight-week Bible study to go with it.

My second goal was that the book would work well for you to read on you own, of course, but also with friends. The best way to tackle these big ideas—hustle, work, rest, and failure—is with other women who can help you have the hard conversations and also celebrate your next best step. I would *love* to see your groups as you gather, so at your first meeting, be sure to take a group photo and share it online.

You can tag me on Instagram **@crystalstine** and use the **#holyhustlebook** hashtag so I can send you some love and encouragement.

HOW TO START A BOOK CLUB

1. Decide what kind of book club you want to host. In real life? Online?

2. Where will you meet? If in real life, will you meet at your home? At a coffee shop? If you're meeting online, will you meet on a blog, in a Facebook group, or on a voice-message app?

3. Determine how often you want to meet. Weekly? Bi-weekly? Monthly?

4. Create a reading schedule, based on how often you'll meet and the number of chapters in your book.

5. Invite friends!

Whether you meet in real life or online, you'll want to invite people far enough in advance for them to have time to purchase the book and make arrangements to join you. You'll also want to share your reading schedule with them so they know what to expect. Are you meeting in real life at each other's homes? Make sure your friends know that and can choose the dates they would like to host!

HOW THIS PLANNER CAN HELP

1. Use the pages titled "My Dreams, Plans, and Goals for the Year" at the beginning of this planner to plan your book club.

2. Schedule your book club meeting dates.

3. Track your reading progress and prayer requests on the weekly pages when you meet.

HOW TO HOST A BOOK CLUB

Invite people over. Read a book. Talk about it.

It's really that simple. You don't need to have a master's degree in hospitality to have friends over to your home. Make sure you have somewhere for people to sit, maybe some extra pens in case someone forgets theirs, and an open door! Snacks and drinks are fine if that brings you joy, but if it adds stress? Skip it! Make this a no-pressure book club and focus on the people you're gathering with, not the party supplies.

Make sure your first gathering is a time to get to know one another. **Here are some questions you can use to get started:**

1. Why is this book interesting to you?
2. What are you hoping to get out of our time together?
3. Have you ever been part of a book club before?
4. What is your all-time favorite book?
5. What book have you started that you couldn't finish (or finished and hated)?

DISCUSSION QUESTIONS

As you're reading the book each week, you'll find dozens of questions sprinkled throughout the text, including a final reflection section at the end. These questions should give you plenty of things to talk about at your meetings, and here are a few more ideas to help get the chatter started:

1. What is the purpose of this book, and who do you believe is the intended audience?

2. Have you read much about this topic before? If so, does the author bring something unique to the subject? If not, did this book pique your interest in the subject?

3. How does this book relate to your life or experiences?

4. Did you connect with the subject? Did it make you want to read more? Did it make you uncomfortable?

5. What Scriptures has God brought to mind as you've been reading?

6. Was there a chapter or passage that stood out for you or led to an aha moment?

7. Has your work or rest changed this week as a result of what you've been reading? If so, how? If not, how would you like it to change?

8. Did this book change your perspective—or maybe even your life? If so, how?

9. What did you learn from this book that you didn't know before?

10. Would you have read this book if it hadn't been a book club selection? Would you recommend reading this book? If so, why?

No matter how perfectly you plan your book club, guess what? Life is going to happen. People will miss meetings, things won't go the way you hoped, the babysitter won't show up, and a random holiday you forgot about will throw everything off.

It's okay.

Encourage everyone in your group to be as consistent as possible. Encourage one another, commit to the reading, extend grace, and have fun! You've got this!

xoxo,

Crystal

The Year in Review

Use this space to reflect on the past year. How did embracing the idea of holy hustle—working hard and resting well—help shape your dreams and goals? What do you hope to add or eliminate from your life next year? What was easy to give back to God, and when was it hard to give Him control of your agenda and plans? What Scripture encouraged you most this year?

_____

_____

_____

_____

_____

_____

_____

_____

_____

_____

_____

_____

_____

_____

_____

_____

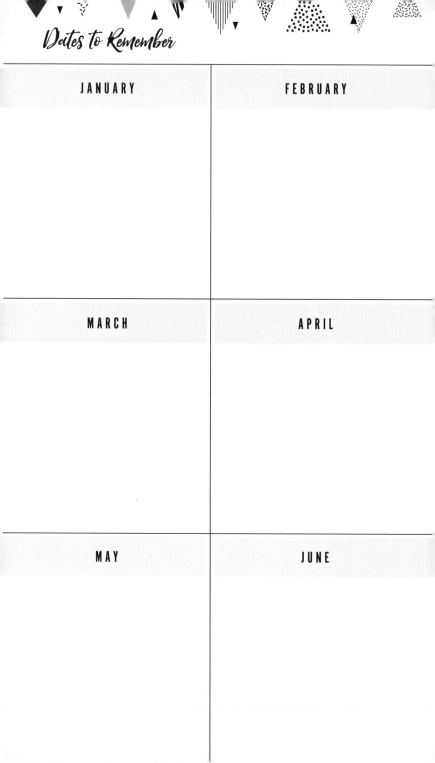

Dates to Remember

JANUARY

FEBRUARY

MARCH

APRIL

MAY

JUNE

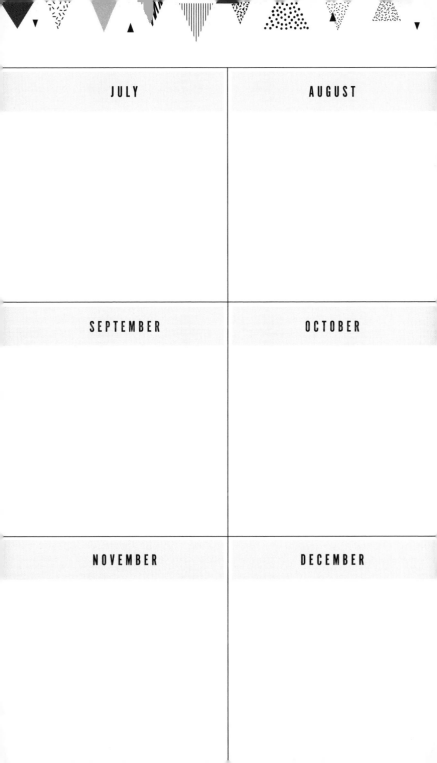

JULY

AUGUST

SEPTEMBER

OCTOBER

NOVEMBER

DECEMBER

NOTES

NOTES

NOTES

NOTES

NOTES

NOTES

NOTES

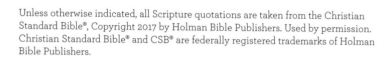

Cover by Kara Klontz Design
Interior Design by Leah Beachy Design
Cover photo © Natalyon / Shutterstock

Holy Hustle Planner
Copyright © 2021 by Crystal Stine
Published by Harvest House Publishers
Eugene, Oregon 97408
www.harvesthousepublishers.com

ISBN 978-0-7369-8231-3 (Milano Softone™)

Printed in China

20 21 22 23 24 25 26 27 28 / RDS—LB / 10 9 8 7 6 5 4 3 2 1